What the Hell

is SEO?

Beginners Guide

(Part One)

Welcome to **What the Hell is SEO?** Part One. The aim of this two-part book is to give web editors and content team members a closer look at SEO tactics, advantages, and tricks. After you read Part One, I suggest you purchase Part Two, the "Advanced Guide". It should be available by December of 2008.

SEO is an abbreviation for **"search engine optimization"**. This is the process that helps your web pages get a higher ranking in search engine results. Of course, a higher ranking correlates with more user traffic and thus more financial success!

Many factors influence search engine optimization (SEO), but the most significant factors are related to your web page content. Therefore, web editors are more involved with SEO than anyone else on your team. If you're editing your pages yourself, you'll find that SEO is not so complicated once you understand how search engines categorize and rank web pages. Plus, you'll better grasp SEO if you follow my step-by-step process.

The first part of this book will introduce you to the outlines and basics of SEO and other aspects of internet business. The second part will introduce you to more advanced techniques and insights.

Please note, this book centers on Google, which has become the internet's dominant search engine. However, the tactics mentioned will also boost your ranking with other search engines.

Enjoy!

Dedication

I dedicate this book to my beautiful son Collin, who just turned 3 years old this September and is currently battling autism. I constantly call him my little angel; he has changed my life more than I've ever dreamed or imagined possible. I love you, buddy!

Today, approximately 1 in 150 individuals are diagnosed with autism, making it more common than pediatric cancer, diabetes, and AIDS combined. So please help the fight! Visit http://www.autismspeaks.org/.

LIMIT OF LIABILITY/DISCLAIMER OF WARRANTY:

Table of Contents

1-Introduction

1.1 Content

2- How do search engines work?

2.1 Google's mechanism

2.2 Keywords repetition

3- How can I get a first-page ranking in Google?

3.1 Text and keywords

3.2 Multimedia and downloadable items

3.2.1 Photos

3.2.1.1 Caption

3.2.1.2 Picture name

3.2.2 Videos and audible executables

3.2.3 Wallpapers

3.3 Hyperlinks

3.4 Profiles

3.5 Meta tags

3.6 Brief and description

3.7 Careful with the spam

4- Gaps between content and development

4.1 Personal experiences

4.2 Team management

5- User-generated content

5.1 Forums

5.1.1 Moderator

5.1.2 Undercover agent!

5.2 YouTube

5.2.1 Embedded code

5.3 UGC Credibility

5.4 Facebook.com

5.5 Wikipedia

5.6 eBay and Amazon

5.7 Amazon

6- Web editor guidelines

6.1 Headlines

6.1.1 Length and clarity

6.2 Subheads

6.3Pull Quotes

6.4 Writing style

6.5 Display tips

6.6 Bylines

6.7 Web editing tips

7-Internet business promotion

7.1 Advertisements

7.2 Live chat

7.3 Sponsors

7.4 Online ads

7.5 Spin-offs

7.6 Newsletters

1-Introduction

For the internet surfer, a search engine is just a handy tool enabling them to find exactly what they are looking for quickly and easily. For portal managers and executives, on the other hand, it's a fundamental way to dramatically increase business.

There are some content-related techniques to follow in order to get a better rank in the results of search engines like **Google**.

Visitors are the core of any website's business. Your site's daily page views (the sum of the surfed pages on your site) are a measurement of your portal's success, and page views are directly related to user density.

SEO (search engine optimization) is among the most beneficial ways of getting and keeping page views high.

Whether you're a web editor, developer, or manager-executive, you should always keep search engine optimization in mind.

Many of your users will find you through search engines. According to Jacob Nielson at www.useit.com, 40% of internet users are search-dominant. That's a substantial number of potential customers!

In addition to bringing in the traffic, SEO techniques have peripheral advantages such as improving usability and aligning content.

This book will introduce you to legitimate and honest basics of optimizing your web pages and getting a higher rank.

It will also give you a glimpse of underhanded tactics, which are not recommended. Consequences of using such techniques are discussed in Part Two.

1.1 Content

Nowadays, even more than design and development, content is the most influential factor affecting a webpage's ranking.

Content includes not only text, but also videos, executables, pictures and everything else users might see or interact with. All of these elements are directly related to SEO.

A site's content must be well-organized and well-optimized to reach its potential. And just imagine your potential! Internet use is rapidly increasing. Internet users increasingly reflect all generations, social classes, and geographical locations, and the best is yet to come.

The majority of global users tend to use Google. The word "Google" has even become a new verb, which is a testament to its dominance.

For this reason, we'll focus on standards and guidelines that are compatible with Google's page ranking mechanism in order to help you obtain a high first-page ranking.

2- How do search engines like Google work?

Optimizing your web pages in accordance with Google's page ranking mechanism will not only help your Google ranking, but will also elevate your rank in other search engines.

Curiously, even some high-profile portals with great traffic do not dedicate enough effort to search engine optimization. No matter how successful your portal is, paying more attention to SEO can boost your success.

2.1 Google's mechanism

When you search for a term with Google, this dominant search engine sends out a software robot or "spider" to check millions of web pages, scrutinizes their content, and almost immediately provide you with a list of the most relevant pages. The order in which results appear depends on the optimization of each page.

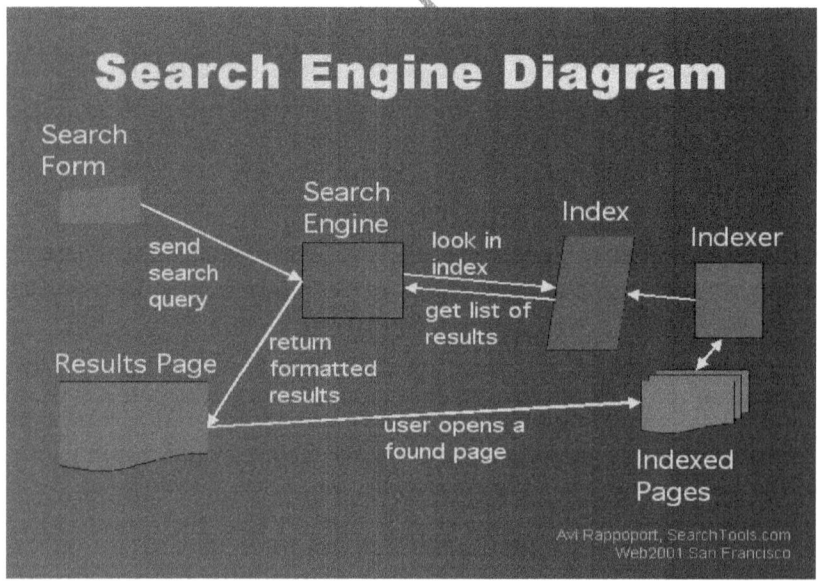

Search Engine Diagram

When the spider first reaches your homepages, it looks for the following:

- Title tags
- Keywords and phrases
- Description
- Meta tags

After that, the spider goes through your other content pages thoroughly, searching for specified keywords and phrases, descriptive meta tags, headings, hyperlinks and alt tag descriptions.

The most important elements to the spider are keywords, headlines, alt tags, link titles, and the alignment among them all.

2.2 Keyword Repetition

Keyword repetition applies not only to articles and news pages, but to all kinds of web pages. For example, I can find some pages just by searching for my own name,

Harry Misner, because it's quite repeated in some pages on the internet:

First result

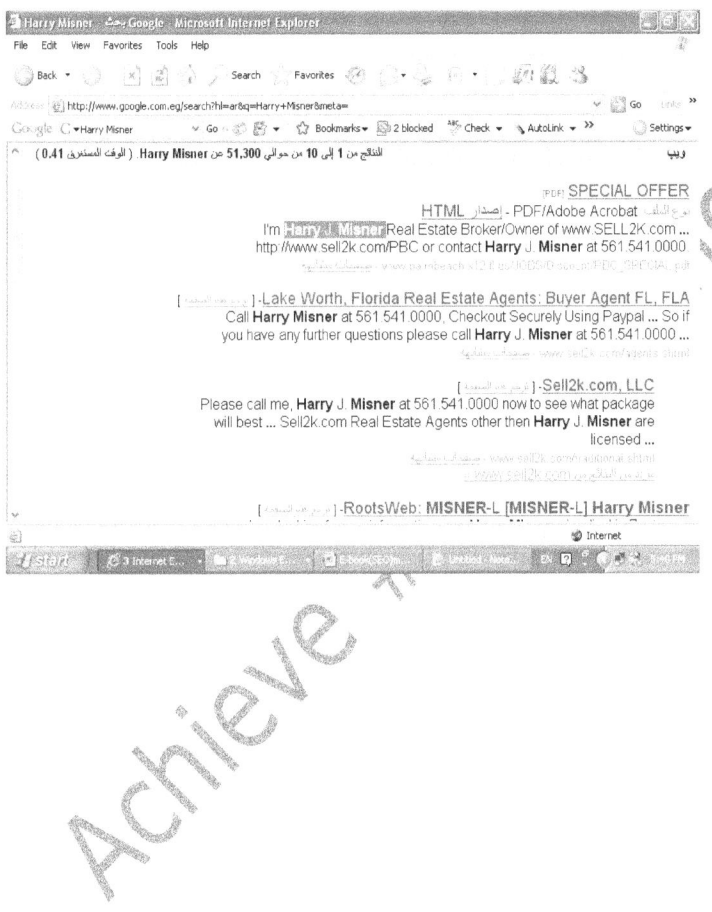

Second result

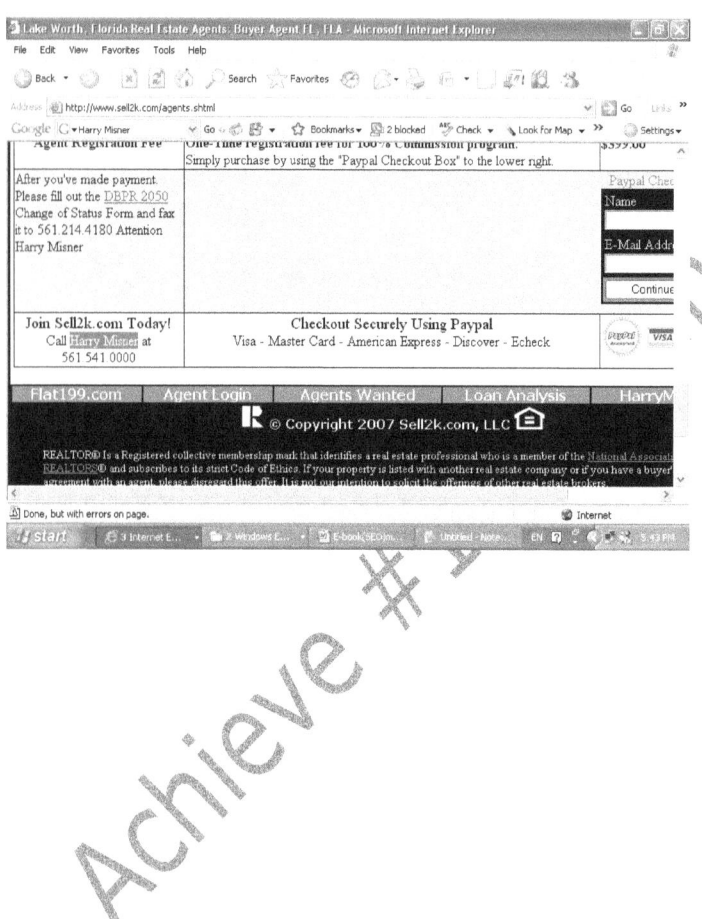

Third result

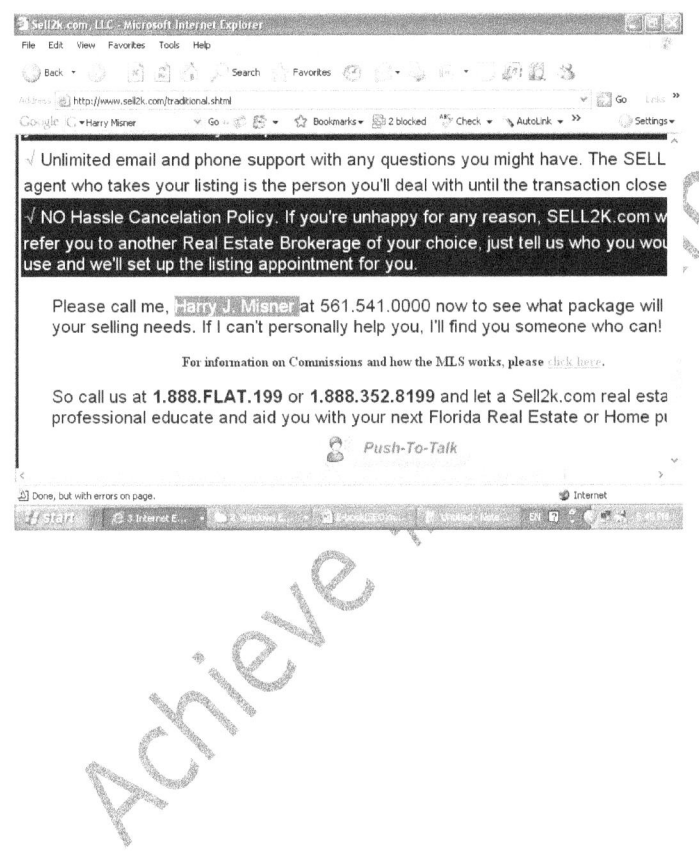

Fourth result

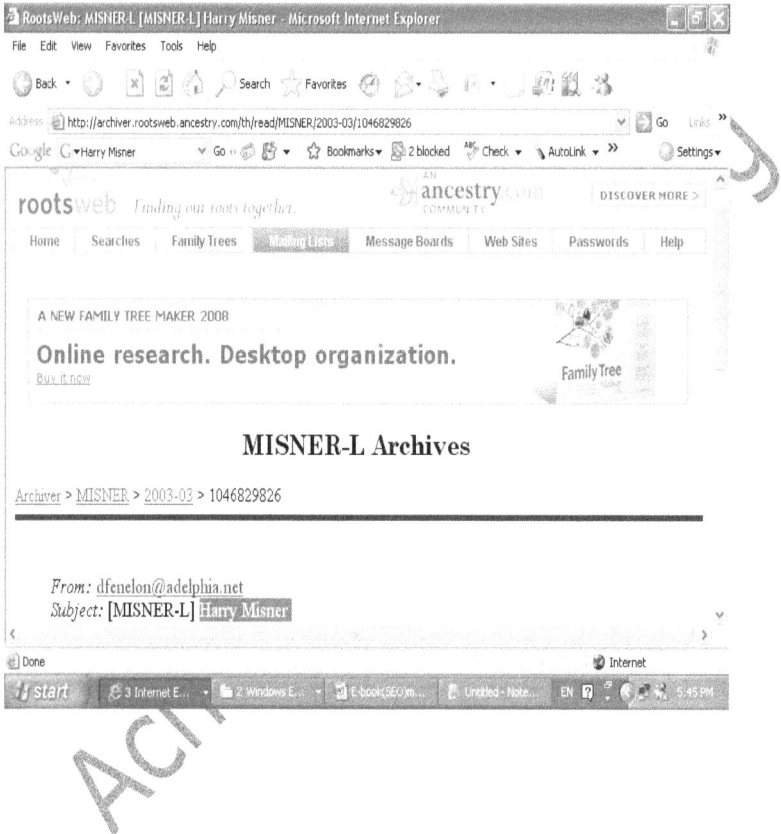

My name, of course, is probably not an appropriate keyword for such pages; I am just trying to make a point: if a word is repeated often enough, it will boost a page's ranking when that word is searched for.

If you manage to repeat an appropriate key word or phrase strategically, along with other optimized content, you'll get satisfactory page rank results. Of course, your competitors are probably doing the same, so the frequent use of keywords alone might not bring drastic results. But be consistent and allow some time to see a boost in traffic.

3- How can you get a first-page rank in Google?

There are many tactics that will help you get a first-page rank in Google. Although they are not difficult, most web editors neglect to use these techniques all the time.

All legitimate content-related tactics go by the name "white-hat SEO tactics". Some of these tactics are related to the writing style in the front end while others apply to the backend, or content that users don't see.

3.1 Text and keywords

Generally, up to five keywords can be extracted from an online article. However, optimization should generally be based on two or three keywords at most.

It is helpful to choose key phrases instead of single words to optimize. One word will usually lead to an official website as a first result, if not completely irrelevant pages.

Besides, users tend to search with key phrases or very specific keywords to find what they are looking for right away.

Once you've chosen your "magic words", repeat them frequently in the text and include them in the headline, subheads, and page name.

For instance, if you focus on the key word "Manchester United" in a five-paragraph news article, it should be repeated about three times, added to the headline, brief and subheads, heading, and page name.

However, repeating these words in the admin keywords field might ruin your SEO; it will be perceived as spam, which usually leads to first page exclusion. Furthermore, excessive repetition of keywords within your text can be considered spam. (More details about that are provided in Part Two.)

You should also consider common misspellings of your key terms. Many users search with wrongly-spelled words, which usually bring misleading results or no results at all!

Examples

"George Bush" might be misspelled as "Jeorge Bush" or "Gorge bsh".

Bin Laden might be misspelled as Ben laden or Benn Ladn.

You can use a special analysis tool to identify common misspellings. (More details about that are provided in Part Two.)

3.2 Multimedia and downloadable items

Online multimedia refers to audio, video, pictures, and wallpapers. It may be essential to some portals and peripheral to others. But like the rest of content elements, your use of multimedia affects your SEO.

3.2.1 Photos

Photos and pictures are probably the most basic sort of multimedia, and they're also the most common across websites.

Sometimes, pictures can help your website to get a first place ranking. This is especially likely if many surfers demand the image. For instance, if you search with the key word "Tom Cruise", you will find that the top Google results are pictures of the American actor.

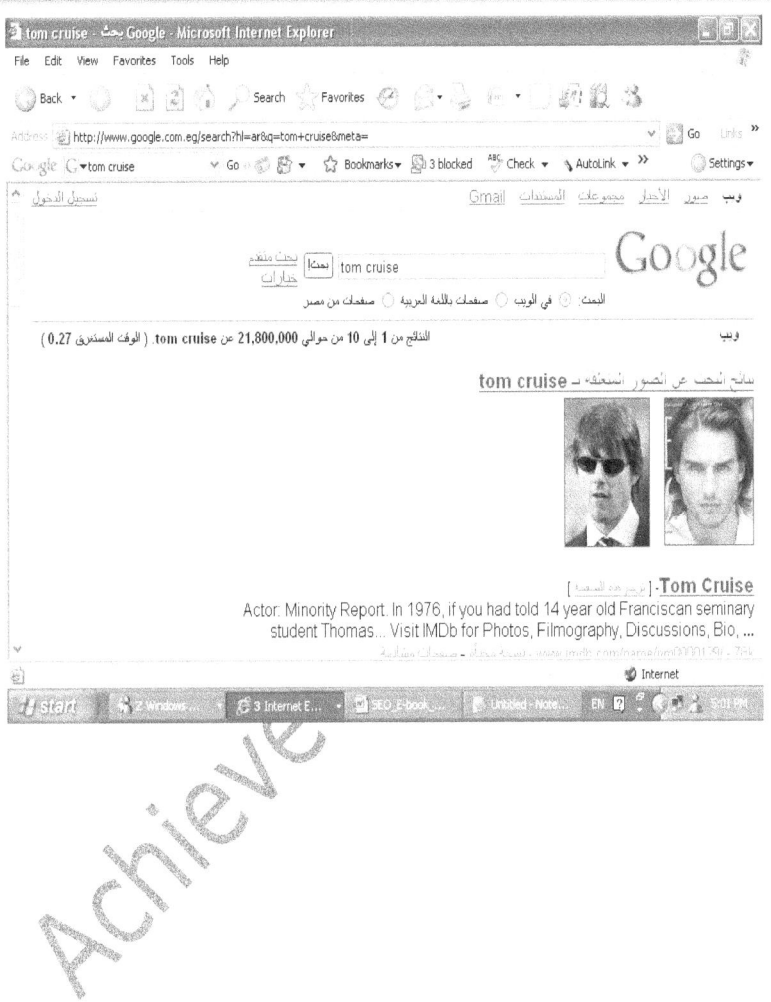

3.2.1.1 Captions

A caption is a very short description of a photo, and it's usually placed below the picture within the article. A caption normally shouldn't exceed five or six words, and you should always try to include your main keywords and phrases.

A photo's caption is important. It has to be relevant and informative. In the news-providing portals, it takes negligible effort to make captions relevant. The caption will naturally relate to the article appearing on the same page.

Remember that a caption is more effective if it is shown on the front end (that is, the part of your site that users see). The photo caption should appear in the photo gallery as well as below each photo or upon hovering with the mouse.

Example

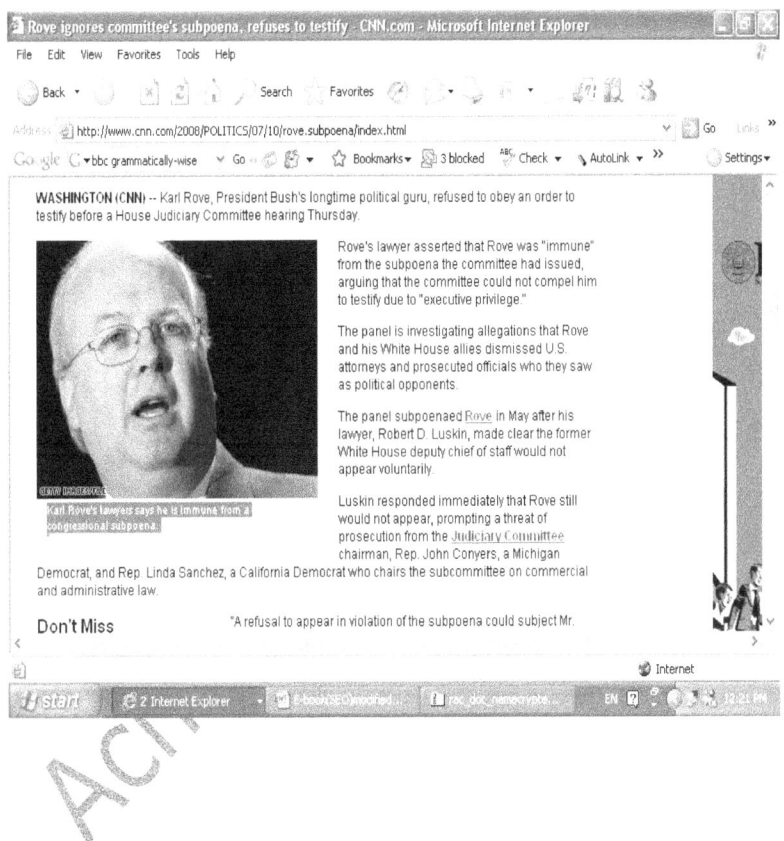

WASHINGTON (CNN) -- Karl Rove, President Bush's longtime political guru, refused to obey an order to testify before a House Judiciary Committee hearing Thursday.

Rove's lawyer asserted that Rove was "immune" from the subpoena the committee had issued, arguing that the committee could not compel him to testify due to "executive privilege."

The panel is investigating allegations that Rove and his White House allies dismissed U.S. attorneys and prosecuted officials who they saw as political opponents.

The panel subpoenaed Rove in May after his lawyer, Robert D. Luskin, made clear the former White House deputy chief of staff would not appear voluntarily.

Luskin responded immediately that Rove still would not appear, prompting a threat of prosecution from the Judiciary Committee chairman, Rep. John Conyers, a Michigan Democrat, and Rep. Linda Sanchez, a California Democrat who chairs the subcommittee on commercial and administrative law.

Karl Rove's lawyers says he is immune from a congressional subpoena.

Don't Miss

"A refusal to appear in violation of the subpoena could subject Mr.

Also note that pictures have to be modified and uploaded with the smallest file size possible, so as to not adversely affect the site's loading time. Of course, you'll need to find a balance between file size and resolution. For this reason, a web editor normally needs to know how to use Adobe Photoshop or another photo processing program. Remember, slow loading might make a potential customer click away to try another site!

3.2.1.2 Picture names

Properly-named pictures should be inserted into articles after every five paragraphs or so. Pictures make the article easier to read and also support SEO.

The best way to name a picture is like this: TonyBlair_98353.jpg.

If it's a two-word name, stick both words together. Capitalize the first letter of the second word. Add an underscore followed by a serial number (that is, the picture ID number, which should be issued automatically by your camera or photo software).

The picture name should be chosen with SEO in mind – not your users. It is only viewable on the back end.

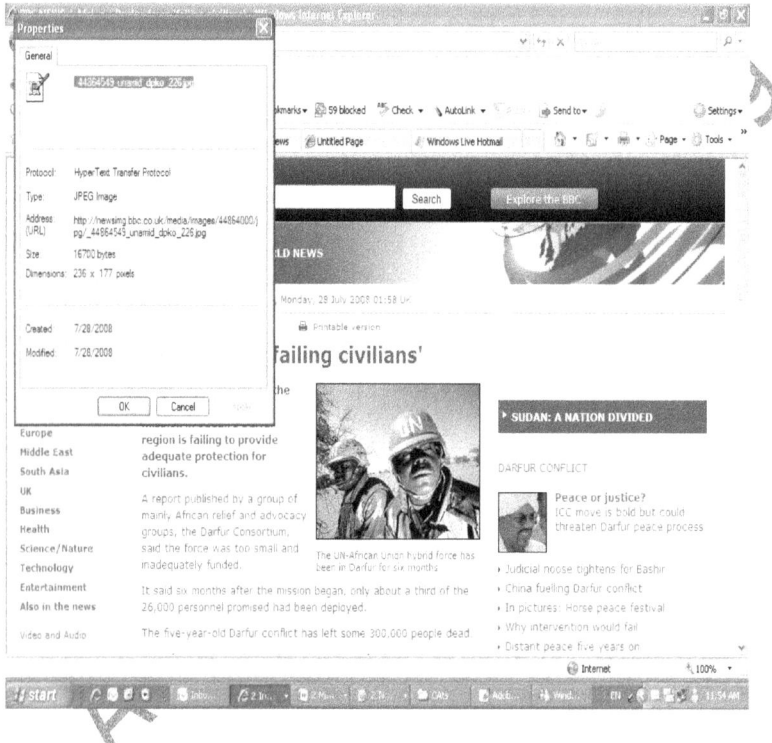

What size pictures should you use? Small-sized pictures are suitable in the middle of the body, floating in the text. It's best NOT to use a wide picture in the middle; that could give a reader the impression that the article is finished when it's not.

3.2.2 Videos and audible executables

Videos and audible executables are another form of online multimedia.

These clips may or may not be downloadable. If they aren't, you'll encourage visitors to return every time they want to watch or listen to your multimedia.

They are preferably added to the bottom of a news web page, and they are named with the same format mentioned for pictures. On the news web pages, multimedia items are usually added in the form of a hyperlink.

There might also be pages of the website devoted entirely to audio and video.

Example text for video hyperlinks

Watch the press conference

Watch the highlights

Bush's latest press release

3.2.3 Wallpapers

Wallpapers generally do not contribute to search engine optimization. The main benefit of wallpaper is the visual attractiveness it adds to your site.

3.3 Hyperlinks

Hyperlinks are very influential in the optimization process. They help the search engine to identify and categorize a page. If the key words within an article are redirecting users to another relevant page, that can help boost your page rankings too. Hyperlinks can help increase your number of page views.

Example

If the article's main keyword is "Bin Laden", then making the word "Bin Laden" clickable to a profile page or to any other Bin Laden-related page will support your SEO.

Another example

If the key word "Manchester United" is linked to Manchester United's profile, it would make it easier for search engines to categorize that page and rank it more highly when that keyword is searched for.

Of course, linking to an *irrelevant* page would have the opposite effect. So be careful when creating hyperlinks. Make sure they are relevant to the original topic, and always check them after publishing.

How long should your hyperlink be? A hyperlink's length is flexible; it can be short, medium or long. It depends on the article's structure and the destination page.

Examples

-Last week, an adviser to the court recommended that it should not shut down the AKP, arguing its decision to lift a ban on Islamic headscarves in universities had not challenged the constitution. (Redirecting to a news page)

- Meanwhile, Turkey - a candidate for the European Union - has pushed its anti-terror campaign on multiple fronts. (Redirecting to a profile page or news page).

- In December 2007, a 24-year-old former missionary candidate killed two people in

suburban Denver, Colorado. (Redirecting to a news page.)

Tip:

Always refer the reader to something at the end of an article through other links. Have a minimum of two hyperlinks at the end of each article. Such links will help boost your SEO.

Note: All links should be in dark vivid blue. That's the color that surfers most associate with clickable links. Also, links should be unified with the rest of your page. That is, they should be made with the same font face or font family. For example, see the following screen shot:

3.4 Profiles

A profile page includes a biography for a player, actor, singer, team, party, dignitary or other individual or entity. It should also contain links to related pages.

For instance, if there is a profile for a particular soccer player, it should contain pictures, game statistics for the current season and previous seasons, relevant team news and so on. Gathering these related pages will help with search engine optimization. The idea is to give your site's visitors a reason to check out your other pages.

Tip

Include a person's birth date or a company's establishment date instead of a particular age. That way, you won't need to make adjustments with time.

3.5 Meta tags

Meta tags can be described as the backbone of a website. They are part of HTML or XHTML codes and are often invisible to users, but they help search engines to specify the web pages much further.

It's a part of the editor's job to write relevant and appropriate meta tags that help the search engine identify the page more easily.

Example

http://www.barcaarabia.com/News/2008/june/BARCELONA-GUARDIOLA-ASSIST.aspx

The red section is in the hands of the editor. He or she has to find a way to effectively describe the whole article with only two or three words. This section may be added to the page's name in the admin or publishing tool.

If your admin does not allow you to write such specific page names or alt tags, but instead assigns an ID number automatically, then you'll need the support of your technical team to override the default.

3.6 Brief and description

A news brief is a summary of a whole article. It is visible to web surfers and should contain all of the article's keywords.

The description, in contrast, is often hidden, and it should be composed of several words only. It's a small summary of the brief.

The headline comes next. Of course, this is even smaller than the description. But try to keep the keywords in the headline, too. Such alignment makes the article more easily found via search engines.

Examples

Brief: The former director of a Dubai jail and 24 wardens and police officers have been sentenced to prison for beating up inmates during a check for drugs.

Description: The former director of a Dubai jail has been sentenced to prison for beating up inmates.

Headline: Dubai jail director sentenced for inmate beatings

Main keywords: Inmate beatings - Dubai jail director

Also try to make the subheads and meta tags related to the main key words. A handy publishing tool called Tridion can assist with this task.

Example of aligned content

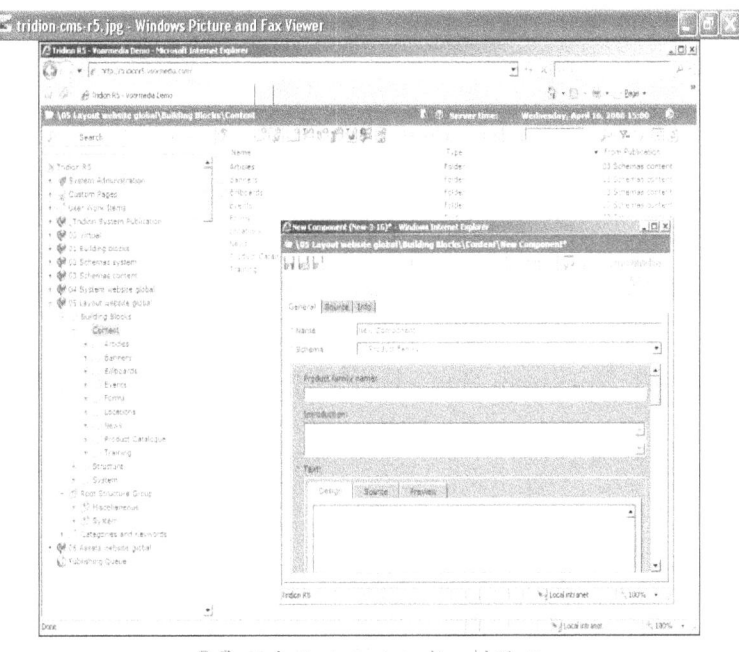

3.7 Careful with the spam

Spam, in a nutshell, is the attempt to trick the relevancy algorithm of a search engine to get a higher rank. It is one of the most common "black hat" SEO tactics, as discussed in Part Two. Even if you use it inadvertently, it can cancel out the effectiveness of all your other SEO efforts! If a search engine detects spamming, it will not grant a high page ranking.

4- Gaps between content and development

When a website is being developed, the content and development teams must develop a strong partnership. The development team contends with all the backstage issues, such as technical errors, making the site compatible with a new feature, and providing the content team with appropriate tools to meet their goals. The content team, of course, deals with the front end.

How is that relevant to SEO? Search engine optimization is one of the content team's main objectives, but it's not such a concern for the techies. So, as an editor or a data entry worker, you must communicate with the developers of your site and inform them of your SEO needs.

Otherwise, the developers may not be aware of how your departments influence one another.

4.1 Personal experiences

I have had a lot of negative experiences with developers, and most of them were due to miscommunication and one-way thinking.

The last thing a developer might think about is how the editor is going to actually use whatever admin or publishing tools they have created. They might just be interested in whether or not a code works, and not its implications for productivity and time management.

For instance, I was once introduced to an admin that required three steps to publish a page, when the task could simply be reduced to only one step. Technical guys simply might not think about an editor's comfort or time frame, so you have to bring that to their attention.

Another example is that the admin that I used to work with had no field for the page description, which is fundamental for SEO. Developers later added it upon our request.

4.3 Team management

All teams have to be **well-managed,** and it helps if workers have close personalized relationships. So as a manager, consider involving your subordinates in social gatherings and other activities. The aim of this is not to turn co-workers into friends, but to make sure they are supportive of each other and cooperate effectively.

It's also very important to respect the organization of workers. That is, every member of the team should know whom to turn to and when.

5- User-generated content (UGC)

User-generated content started becoming very popular in 2005. Blogs and online forums are good examples. These sites may be entirely user-generated. If a site is entirely user-generated, then the entire site's content is in the hand of the users; there are no editors on a content team. The registered users play the role of web editor, and they also intervene in the SEO process.

Other sites with user-generated content have less input from the public. For example, they might be limited to a few comments that readers add to the posted articles.

In any case, the main concerns of such sites' owners is to supervise the posted materials regularly to ensure that users only post appropriate material. If the site is almost entirely user-generated, you'll want to guide users so that they use SEO tactics effectively.

5.1 Forums

Forums are online rooms where people meet to discuss particular topics or to buy and sell goods.

Online forums mainly depend on community building. The more you have a spirit of community, the more attached members will become, and the more your forum site will thrive.

5.1.1 Moderators

Every forum should have one or more moderators who keep an eye on contributions and make sure that all postings are legitimate.

Moderators have the authority to warn and expel members who cross the line with abusive postings. Each forum should display its terms of use to make sure there won't be any misunderstandings about what is acceptable.

Once you have established a forum site, you might be able to turn your moderating work over to a member. If the forum is popular, then finding a moderator who will work for *free* won't be a problem at all! To the contrary, users will look forward to taking up such a post. Simply try to motivate members to compete with each other for this job. For example, you could announce that the user with the highest posting rate is going to be appointed as a moderator.

5.1.2 Undercover agents!

There is an old well-known trick in which someone from the content team or a forum founder pretends to be a member of the forum. This can help encourage interaction on the site. This "undercover" member can also help informally guide other users to use SEO tactics.

5.2 YouTube

The powerhouse Youtube.com may be the most thriving user-generated content site in the world. Millions of registered users from all over the globe upload videos in a wide variety of categories. The site's content team has almost no involvement in designing the content. They just supervise the uploaded videos in order to make sure none of the users violate the site's terms and conditions. If a user does violate such terms, the video will be removed and the user might be banned. For example, see the screenshot on the next page.

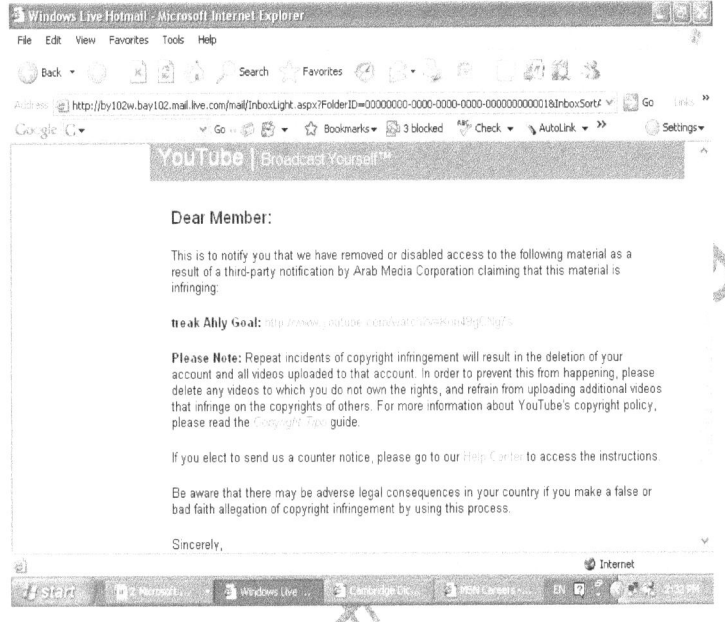

This is a somewhat aggressive warning in response to a user uploading copyrighted material from television broadcast. It's not an automated mail; as you can see, the moderator mentioned the precise case and added the link of the video.

How does SEO relate to YouTube's users? Smart use of SEO tactics can help make a user's videos more popular and easier to find. Specifically, the uploader should choose the most appropriate key words and phrases for their video.

5.2.1 Embedded code

Embedded code allows other websites to add videos from YouTube or other similar sites to their own pages.

This helps both parties. The site has the privilege of providing its users with YouTube videos, and YouTube further consolidates its domination.

Check the next print screen for embedded code.

This print screen shows a YouTube video added to another site.

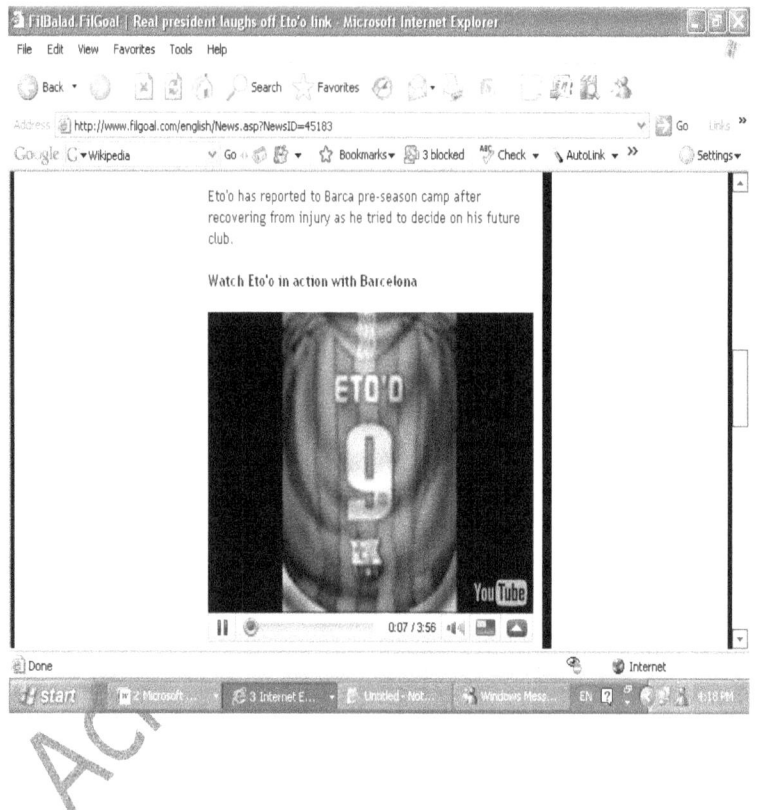

5.3 UGC Credibility

User-generated content has received a lot of criticism because there is no guarantee concerning credibility. Users can post false news or hoax photos of a high-profile official. Webmasters have no legal obligations to authenticate information; users are free to write whatever they want.

However, blogs are often considered good sources for news. Even if somebody posts something inaccurate, someone else will come along to publicly refute them.

5.4 Facebook.com

Facebook is a wonderful example of world-wide community building. The portal has become one of the most popular in the world! It allows each user to create a personal profile and link to their friends' profiles. It also has numerous gadgets and features,

such as birthday reminders and online word games.

SEO is not so relevant to members' profiles, but it might be important for Facebook groups. Such groups are exactly like separate sites. The founders of the groups are the only ones entitled to alter or modify their pages. And if they want more members, they need to be aware of SEO!

If a Facebook.com group is well-optimized, it will get a high ranking like any other website.

5.5 Wikipedia

Wikipedia is one of the most visited online encyclopedias in the whole world. It was launched in 2001, and it's another example of a successful UGC-based site.

Wikipedia aims to provide internet users with a wide range of knowledge in dozens of languages. Although the information is

provided by the public, Wikipedia has managed to maintain high credibility. Users are vigilant about deleting inaccurate information and making sure that relevant facts are included. A history of each article's revisions can be viewed at any time.

Wikipedia owes its success in part to great optimization. For one thing, each encyclopedia entry tends to have dozens of links to other Wikipedia articles or relevant information elsewhere on the web.

This example on the following page shows the results for a simple one-word search – Lampard – and Wikipedia achieved the third result, just after the athlete's official site.

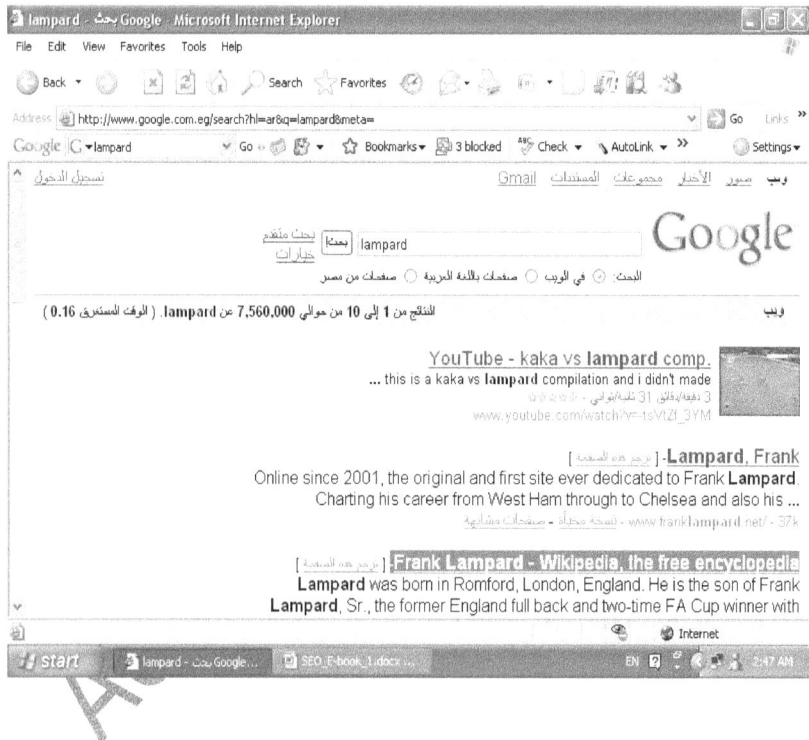

5.6 eBay and Amazon

EBay.com is another major website with user-generated content. It conducts online auctions and facilitates the buying and purchasing of goods. The company was founded in 1995. By 2007, eBay's annual revenue exceeded $7 billion!

Amazon.com, an e-commerce business based in Washington, is another example of a successful online business with user-generated content. The company was founded in 1994 and launched its online presence a year later as an online bookstore. By now, Amazon has diversified to provide a wide range of goods, from books and DVDs to apparel and furniture.

In both cases, corporate success has been facilitated by great SEO and the establishment of mutual trust between site moderators and users.

6-Web editor guidelines

Effective web editing brings the dual rewards of gaining you a great page ranking and keeping your visitors engaged. Below are some tips for online editing.

6.1 Headlines

There is a trade-off between applying SEO techniques and sticking to basics of traditional journalism.

It's important for a traditional newspaper headline to be eye-catching, exciting or a bit off-beat to attract readers. However, Google's domination set new rules, which oblige the content team to stop thinking as journalists, and rather think as web editors.

The headline has to be **informative** and **to the point**, avoiding ambiguity.

The headline has to speak for itself and leave no doubt that this article is the right one to click on. This is especially important when the headline must be chosen from a list of search results, without a photo right there to confirm what the story is about. Any tabloid-style headline might confuse the user and make him or her skip your page.

For the sake of SEO, a web headline might need to sacrifice creativity for clarity. For example, a newspaper article about Britney Spears' second pregnancy might be headlined "Oops! She did it again." But for web optimization, a better choice would be the unambiguous choice: "Britney Spears' second baby on the way."

6.1.1 Length

Headlines should be limited to seven or eight words. The last part of a long headline might not appear in search engine results, and this particular part might contain the most important information!

Example

-<u>United Airways likely to order up to 100 planes in July</u> This is a sort of print news headline; it is quite long and close to a short summary.

For online use, this sort of headline should be edited into fewer words:

-<u>United Airways might order up to 100 planes</u>

Even eliminating just one word can be beneficial:

-I will resign soon, says Bush

-I will resign soon - Bush

To further illustrate the importance of the headline's length, I searched Google with the key phrase "Deoc in Chelsea" once I knew that the player had sealed a deal with the London-based club.

*T*he *Guardian* was ranked third, appearing on the first page of Google's results. However, because of headline decisions, the BBC's coverage did not appear until the third page of results!

Only the first three words of the titles were viewable, which were not nearly enough for SEO.

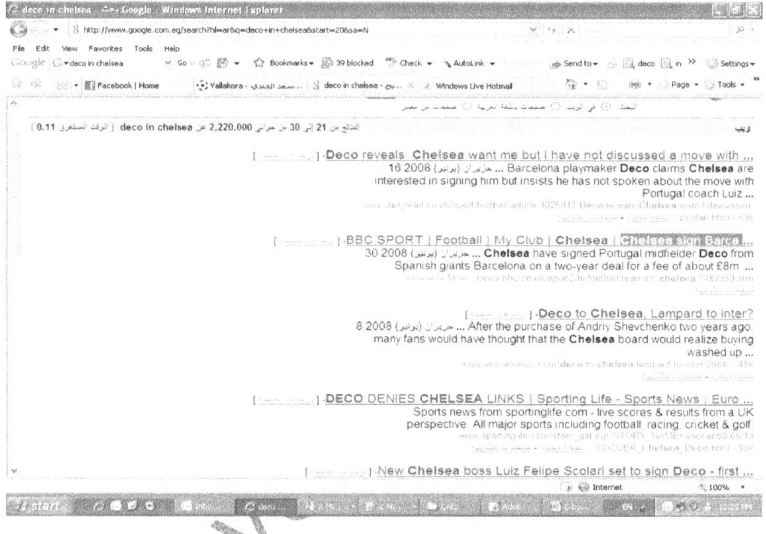

In print newspapers, two-part headlines are common. Because of length concerns, however, two-part headers are not so effective when used online.

Example

-Bryant to join Chicago Bulls; O'Neil close to retiring

Try not to merge two important events together in one article. It would be better if you focused on only one event per headline. Consider dividing the story into two separate articles for online use.

6.4 Subheads

Subheads are desirable in lengthy articles. They help with organization and keep your readers engaged.

Subheads should be shorter than headlines, usually consisting of two or three words.

Ideally, subheads will use your keywords. This will increase your chances of obtaining a high page rank.

Subheads are usually written in **bold** in the same color as the rest of the article, and are preceded by a single line space. Some sites write their subheads with capital letters using the same font of the text.

Example of bold subheads

What the Hell is SEO

by Harry J. Misner

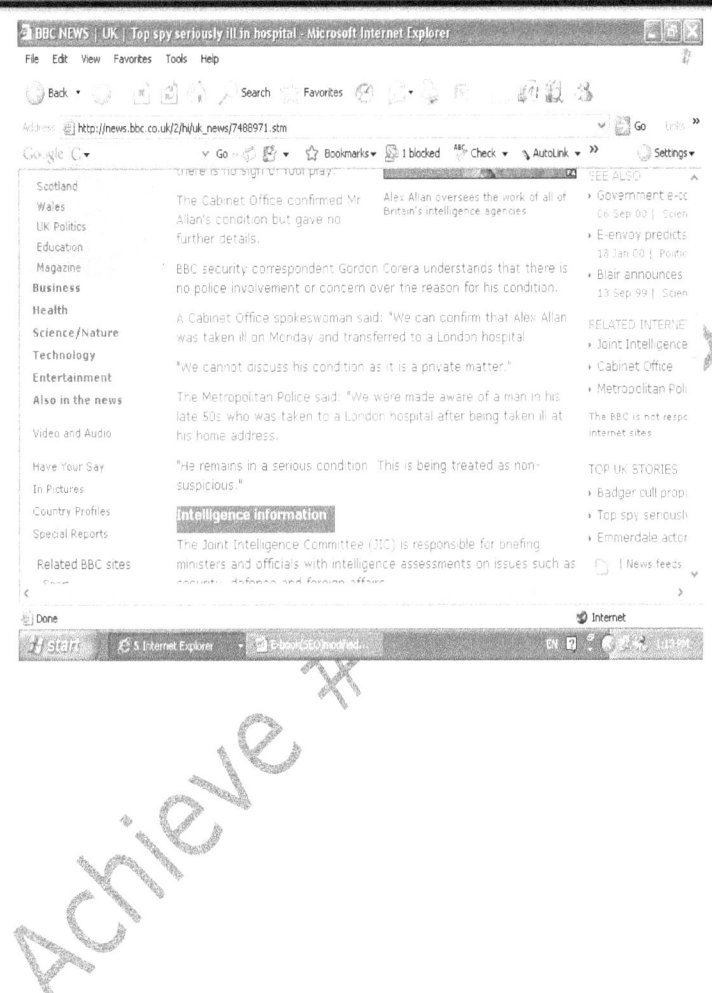

Example of capitalized subheads

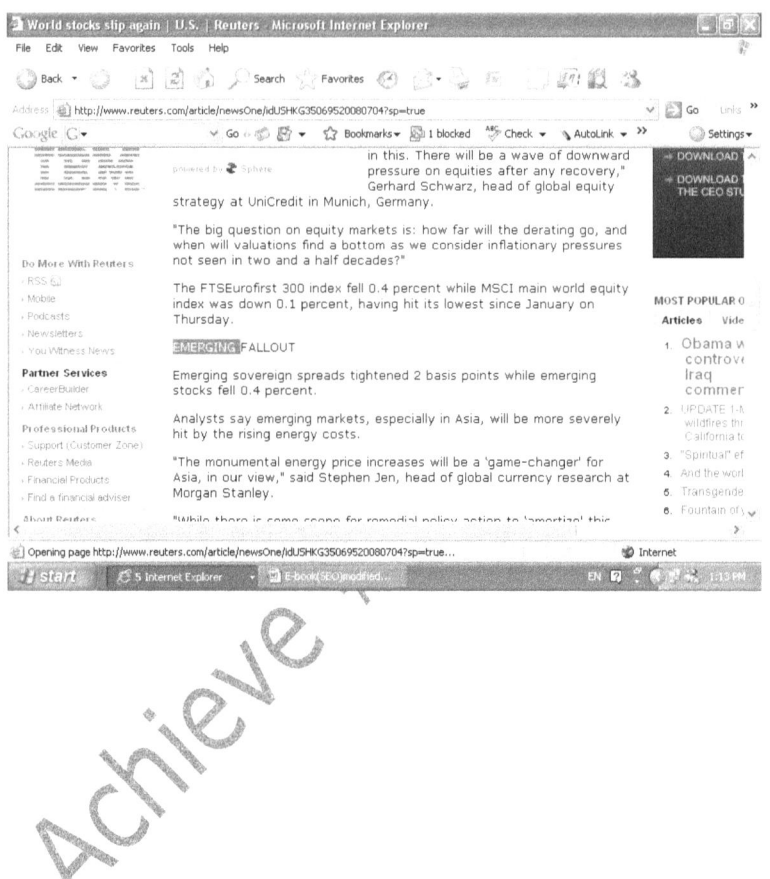

6.5 Pull Quotes

Pull quotes are article excerpts that summarize what the article is all about. You can normally use at least one pull quote per article, and in lengthy articles, one per five or six paragraphs. (However, a small picture can be exchanged for a pull quote. The idea is just to somehow break up large texts.)

A pull quote should contain a maximum of 15 words. Write the quote with the same font face and color of the article text, but in bold and 2 sizes larger. Also use quotation marks and perhaps a different background color to help the quote stand out.

6.6 Writing style

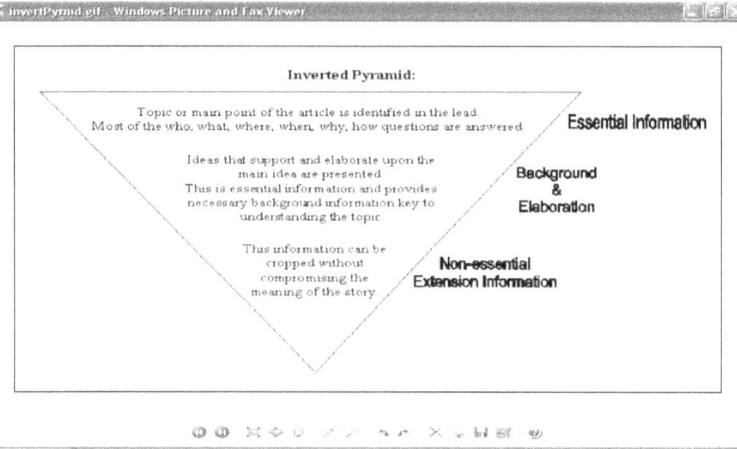

Online and offline media may use different writing styles.

The inverted pyramid is generally the best way to write news stories, whether online or off. That is, begin with the most important information and funnel down to the less important details:

According to research, a person who usually read 100 words in a printed magazine would read only 40 words in an online publication. So, consider writing shorter paragraphs than those find offline. Small paragraphs might help keep the reader, especially when a smaller font must be used and could be hard on their eyes. In fact, it's not uncommon for online articles to limit a paragraph to just one sentence.

The use of shorter sentences has the SEO benefit of letting you strategically repeat keywords without boring the reader.

6.7 Display tips

- Generally, the whole article should not exceed 600 words, and the page length shouldn't exceed three mouse scrolls.

-To make reading and scanning easier, make sure there is a high contrast between the text color and the background. (The most common combination is black text on a white background.)

-Do not use Italics except for names of movies, albums, books or songs.

-Do not underline any words or phrases in the text that are not <u>hyperlinked.</u>

6.8 Bylines

A byline is the name of the writer or editor. In print news, the byline appears before the story begins. Some web portals reveal the names of their writers and editors, while others do not.

Online bylines should be written in the same font color and size as the article/paragraph. They may or may not be made bold.

Examples

On-site coverage: *Reported By*

Analysis articles: *Written By*

Research (full coverage): *Compiled By*

Entertainment pieces: *By*

6.9 Web editing tips

- Note that words like "today", "yesterday" and "tomorrow" should be avoided. Instead, use the date or name of the day. Some search engine results do not show the date of the article, so ambiguous words like "today" can be confusing.

-Try to adopt one writing style for all the portal's content (e.g., formal, informal, hip)

-Appoint proofreaders to review each piece before publication. If hiring proofreaders is not an option, have editors revise each other's work.

7-Internet business

As long as you occupy an internet-related position, it's very important to understand how websites can be profitable. In general, all sites increase profits by increasing their number of users. The following are the most common approaches to increasing traffic.

7.1 Advertisements

Traditional magazine and newspaper advertisements can be helpful in attracting visitors to your site. Too many webmasters forget about advertising in the "real world"!

7.2 Live chat

A great way to gain popularity is to host a celebrity and let him or her interact with your visitors. You will play the role of mediator in that process, conveying questions and answers. This sort of event can add instant prestige to your site! Moreover, it's a good way to attract media attention.

7.3 Sponsors

The majority of well-established sites are powered by sponsors. Once you have demonstrated your ability to gain traffic, a sponsor may pay to have their banner and/or products appear on your site. This will, in turn, attract more users. Just be sure that your sponsor's product or service is relevant to your visitors' lives.

For example, in the print screen that follows, an athletic academy is sponsoring a sports website.

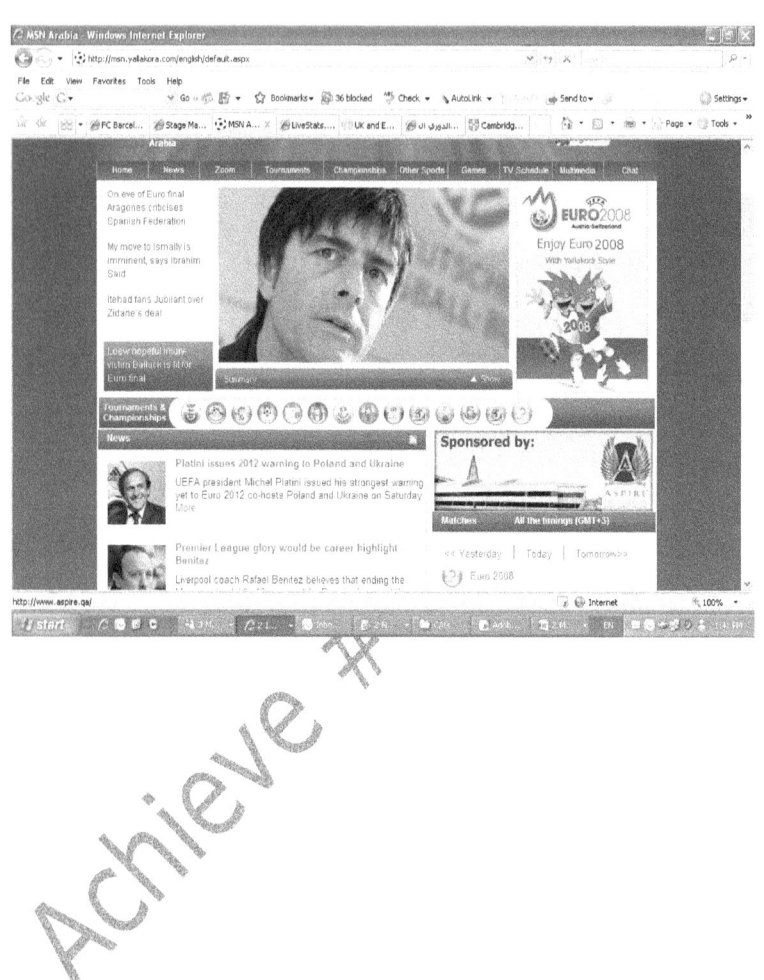

7.4 Online ads

There are two main types of online advertising. One targets any visitor, and the other reaches an established list of users.

The first is based on daily page views, or the sum of the surfed pages on your site. The higher your page views, the more you can charge for ad space.

The second kind relies on an email list that you've collected through your site. If you can offer an advertiser a spot in an email message, and can guarantee sending that email to 500,000 active users, you have a great way to get paid!

7.5 Spin-offs

Portal spin-offs are usually produced for promotional purposes and don't directly contribute to portal revenue. Such products might include T-shirts with a site logo or a colorful schedule of sporting events. The products themselves might not bring a great profit, but they help promote name recognition.

7.6 Newsletters

Newsletters may be provided to registered users to inform them of your site's latest updates. It's a good way to keep in touch with active users, and also a way to bring back old customers. You might send out a newsletter regularly on a predictable schedule, or more infrequently to inform people about specific updates or features.

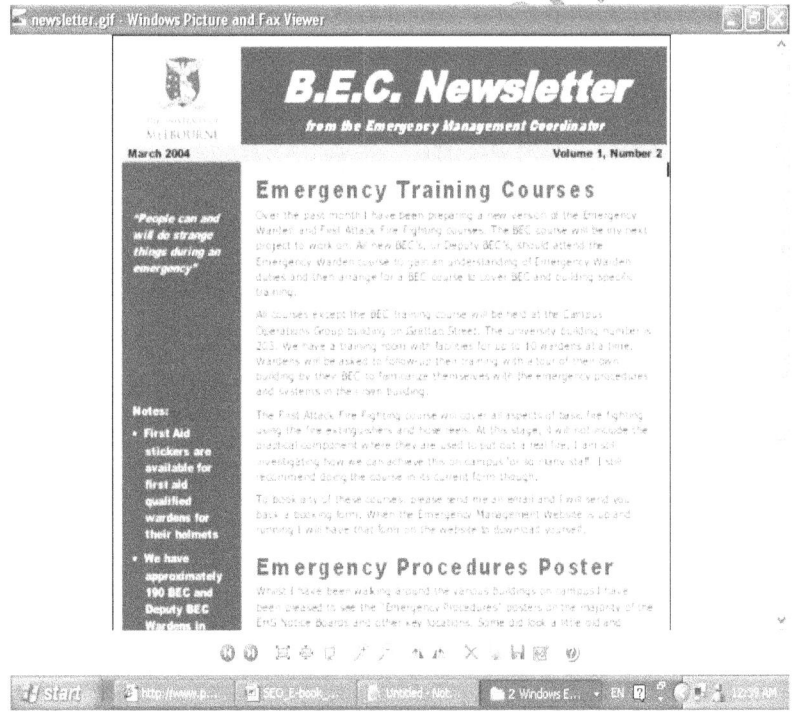

FREE BONUS

Once my new website is finished being designed, everyone who purchases my books will be granted lifetime access using the login information below:

http://www.harrymisner.com/google

username: customer

password: appreciation

Here you'll be able to ask me any questions you might have via email and purchase updated or additional books & eBooks at a discounted rate.

"God Bless to all My Family & Friends. You are always in my prayers whether I tell you daily or not"

Harry J. Misner